Grayslake Area Public Library District
Grayslake, Illinois

1. A fine will be charged on each book which is not returned when it is due.

2. All injuries to books beyond reasonable wear and all losses shall be made good to the satisfaction of the Librarian.

3. Each borrower is held responsible for all books drawn on his card and for all fines accruing on the same.

First
Facts®

UNEXPLAINED MYSTERIES

The Unsolved Mystery of ATLANTIS

by Michael Martin

CAPSTONE PRESS
a capstone imprint

First Facts are published by Capstone Press,
1710 Roe Crest Drive, North Mankato, Minnesota 56003
www.capstonepub.com

Library of Congress Cataloging-in-Publication Data
Cataloging-in-publication information is on file with the Library of Congress.
ISBN 978-1-4765-3096-3 (library binding)
ISBN 978-1-4765-3427-5 (eBook PDF)
ISBN 978-1-4765-3441-1 (paperback)

Editorial Credits
Anna Butzer, editor; Juliette Peters, designer; Wanda Winch, media researcher;
Kathy McColley, production specialist

Photo Credits
Alextooth.com, 10; The Bridgeman Art Library: ©Look and Learn, 9, © Look and Learn/Private Collection/ Roger Payne, 4, 16; Corbis: Reuters, 19; excerpt from Ignatius Donnelly's book Atlantis: *The Antediluvian World*, 12; Getty Images: Lonely Planet Images/Michael Lawrence, 14; Image by Erebus: erebus-art.com, 6-7; Shutterstock: Linda Bucklin, cover, 1, Regissercom, 20-21, sgrigor, design element, zeber, design element

Printed in the United States of America in North Mankato.
032013   007223CGF13

Table of Contents

Chapter 1

Plato (left) first heard the Atlantis story in Greece.

The Lost City of the Sea

y001.94
Mar
12.13

A famous Greek named Solon went to Egypt in 600 BC. In Egypt he heard about the sinking of an island city called Atlantis. Solon told the story about Atlantis when he came back to Greece. The Greek **philosopher** Plato heard the story that had traveled from Egypt. Plato wrote down the story about this **mysterious** island around 360 BC.

philosopher—a person who studies truth and knowledge

mysterious—hard to explain or understand

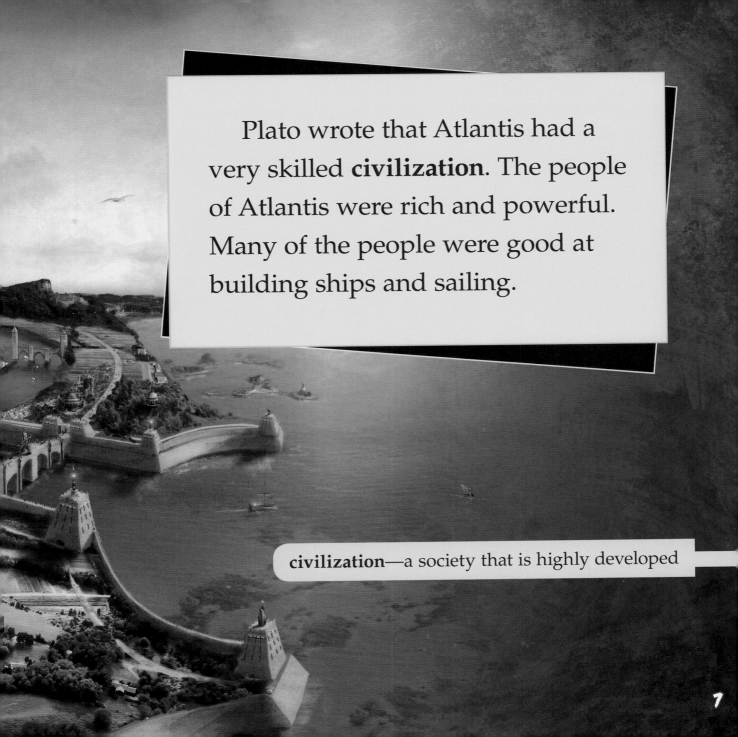

Plato wrote that Atlantis had a very skilled **civilization**. The people of Atlantis were rich and powerful. Many of the people were good at building ships and sailing.

civilization—a society that is highly developed

Plato's story says the people of Atlantis started to fight with other civilizations. They attacked the city of Athens, Greece. After the Atlanteans lost to Athens, a great **earthquake** hit Atlantis. Huge waves crashed into the island. Soon the whole city was underwater.

If Atlantis was real it might be filled with many treasures.

earthquake—the sudden shaking of Earth's surface

Chapter 2

History and Legend

People have wondered for more than 2,000 years if Atlantis was a real place. Some people believe that Plato made up the story of Atlantis to teach a lesson. But Plato **insisted** that Atlantis was real. Many people believe him and continue to search for it.

insist—to demand something very firmly

CHAPTER V.

THE TESTIMONY OF THE SEA.

SUPPOSE we were to find in mid-Atlantic, in front of the Mediterranean, in the neighborhood of the Azores, the remains of an immense island, sunk beneath the sea—one thousand miles in width, and two or three thousand miles long—would it not go far to confirm the statement of Plato that, "beyond the strait where you place the Pillars of Hercules, there was an island larger than Asia (Minor) and Libya combined," called Atlantis? And suppose we found that the Azores were the mountain peaks of this drowned island, and were torn and rent by tremendous volcanic convulsions; while around them, descending into the sea, were found great strata of lava; and the whole face of the sunken land was covered for thousands of miles with volcanic débris, would we not be obliged to confess that these facts furnished strong corroborative proofs of the truth of Plato's statement, that "in one day and one fatal night there came mighty earthquakes and inundations which ingulfed that mighty people? Atlantis disappeared beneath the sea; and then that sea became inaccessible on account of the quantity of mud which the ingulfed island left in its place."

And all these things recent investigation has proved conclusively. Deep-sea soundings have been made by ships of different nations; the United States ship *Dolphin*, the German frigate *Gazelle*, and the British ships *Hydra*, *Porcupine*, and *Challenger* have mapped out the bottom of the Atlantic, and the result is the revelation of a great elevation, reaching from a point on the coast of the British Islands southwardly to the coast of South America, a

MAP OF ATLANTIS, WITH ITS ISLANDS AND CONNE[CTING] SOUNDINGS.

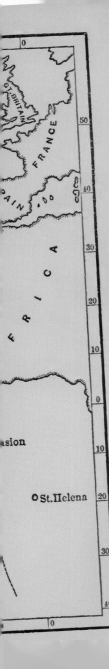

A United States congressman named Ignatius Donnelly wrote a book about Atlantis in 1882. He wrote that people from around the world tell stories of a huge flood. Donnelly believed these **legends** were really memories of the same flood that sunk Atlantis.

legend—a story passed down from earlier times that could seem believable

Chapter 3

Studying Possible Locations

If Atlantis was real, the biggest mystery is where it was. Some people think it was near the Bahamas or Spain.

Others believe it was near Bimini Island in the Caribbean Sea. A stone block path was found on the ocean floor near the island in 1968. The path became known as Bimini Road. Some people believe the road could be part of Atlantis.

True or False?

Is Bimini Road proof that Atlantis existed?

True:
The stone blocks found in the Caribbean Sea look like they are human-made. They are shaped like squares.

False:
Scientists say that sometimes beach rock breaks into square-shaped blocks. They believe Bimini Road is a natural rock formation.

True:
Some researchers exploring Bimini Road have found stones with odd holes in them.

False:
Scientists say that some sea animals can create holes through rocks. They do not think these markings were made by an old civilization.

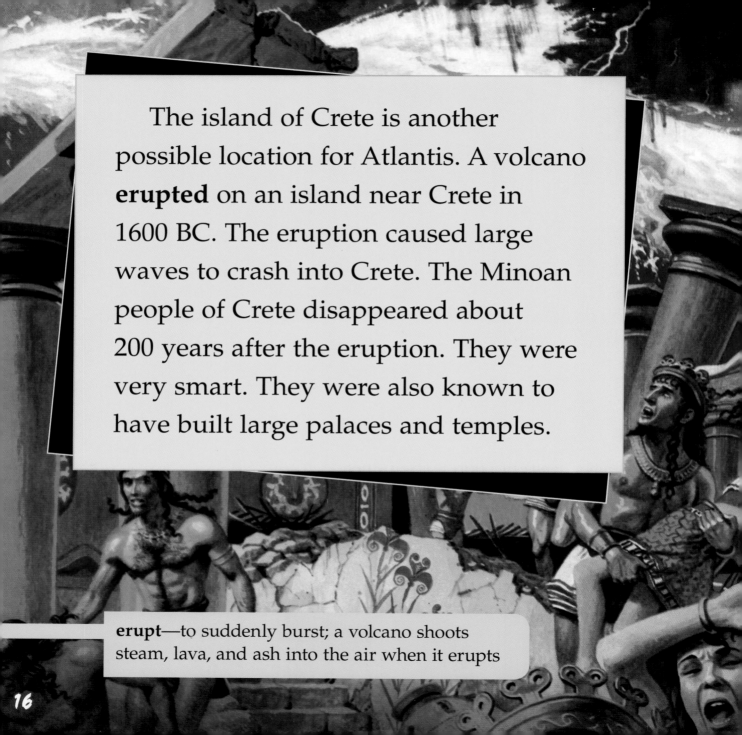

The island of Crete is another possible location for Atlantis. A volcano **erupted** on an island near Crete in 1600 BC. The eruption caused large waves to crash into Crete. The Minoan people of Crete disappeared about 200 years after the eruption. They were very smart. They were also known to have built large palaces and temples.

erupt—to suddenly burst; a volcano shoots steam, lava, and ash into the air when it erupts

Was Atlantis Antarctica?

True:

Some people say Atlantis was Antarctica. They base this belief on studies by Professor Charles Hapgood. He studied old sea maps from the 1500s. Hapgood believed the maps were copied from much older maps. He thought the maps showed the edge of Antarctica. But Antarctica was not discovered until the 1800s. Hapgood thought people lived on Antarctica at a time when it was ice-free and warmer.

False:

Antarctica has been buried under ice sheets for millions of years. Most researchers think that Atlantis existed about 12,000 years ago.

True:

Believers say it is possible that objects from an ancient civilization may be buried under Antarctica's ice.

False:

No proof of ancient people living on Antarctica has ever been found.

Chapter 4

Searching for Answers

Plato might have been wrong about the size and location of Atlantis. Scientists found that the Egyptian symbol for 100 looks a lot like the Greek symbol for 1,000. It is possible that Plato's numbers were all 10 times too large. Because of this **theory**, people continue to look for Atlantis all over the world.

Egyptian 100	Greek 1,000
℮	,α

theory—an idea that explains something that is unknown

British historian Jim Allen believes Atlantis was located where present-day Quillacas is. This area in southern Spain was once covered by large lakes and inland seas.

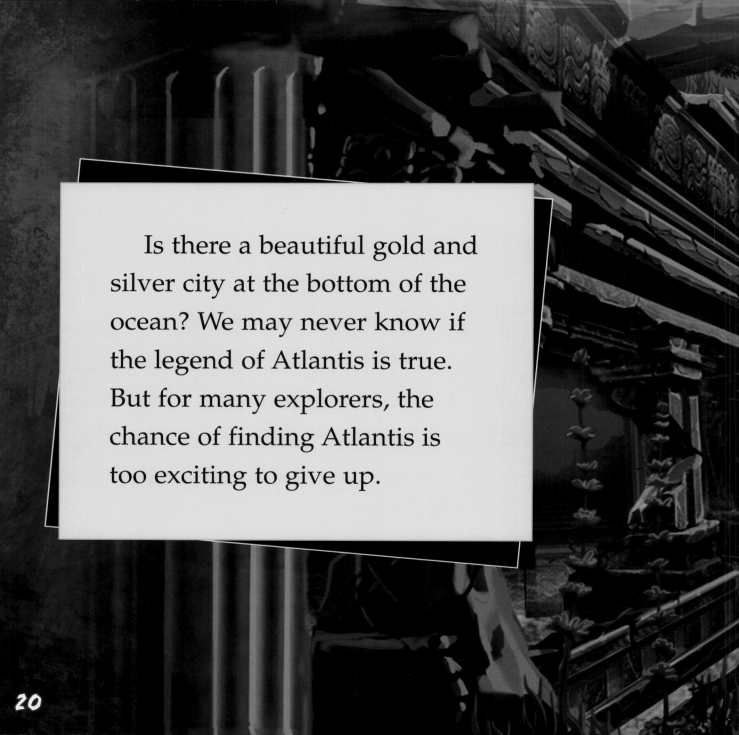

Is there a beautiful gold and silver city at the bottom of the ocean? We may never know if the legend of Atlantis is true. But for many explorers, the chance of finding Atlantis is too exciting to give up.

Glossary

civilization (si-vuh-ly-ZAY-shuhn)—a society that is highly developed

earthquake (UHRTH-kwayk)—the sudden shaking of Earth's surface

erupt (i-RUHPT)—to suddenly burst; a volcano shoots steam, lava, and ash into the air when it erupts

insist (in-SIST)—to demand something very firmly

legend (LEJ-uhnd)—a story passed down from earlier times that could seem believable

mysterious (miss-TIHR-ee-uhss)—hard to explain or understand

philosopher (fuh-LOSS-uh-fer)—a person who studies truth and knowledge

theory (THEE-ur-ee)—an idea that explains something that is unknown

Read More

Michels, Troy. *Atlantis.* The Unexplained. Minneapolis: Bellwether Media, 2011.

Troupe, Thomas Kingsley. *The Legend of Atlantis.* Legend Has It. Mankato, Minn.: Picture Window Books, 2012.

Walker, Kathryn. *The Mystery of Atlantis.* Unsolved! New York: Crabtree Pub. Co., 2010.

Internet Sites

FactHound offers a safe, fun way to find Internet sites related to this book. All of the sites on FactHound have been researched by our staff.

Here's all you do:

Visit *www.facthound.com*

Type in this code: 9781476530963

Super-cool stuff!

Check out projects, games and lots more at
www.capstonekids.com

Index